FOR

FROM

DATE

Poems for My Valentine

A GIFT OF LOVE

WATERCOLORS BY
GAIL ROTH

IDEALS PUBLICATIONS, A DIVISION OF GUIDEPOSTS
NASHVILLE, TENNESSEE

ISBN 0-8249-4124-1

Published by Ideals Publications, a division of Guideposts
535 Metroplex Drive, Suite 250
Nashville, Tennessee 37211
www.idealspublications.com

Caseside printed in the U.S.A.
Text printed and bound in Mexico.
Printed by R.R. Donnelley & Sons.

Library of Congress Cataloging-in-Publication Data

Poems for my valentine: a gift of love/watercolors by Gail Roth
    p. cm.
    Includes index
    ISBN 0-8249-4124-1 (alk.paper)
    1. Love poetry, American. 2. Love poetry, English. 3. Valentine's Day--Poetry.

    PS595.L6 P64 2001
    811.008'03543--dc21   2001024622

10 8 6 4 2 1 3 5 7 9

POEMS SELECTED BY PATRICIA A. PINGRY
DESIGNED BY EVE DEGRIE

ACKNOWLEDGMENTS

CROWELL, GRACE NOLL. "When I Think of You" from *Bright Harvest*. Copyright © 1952 by Grace Noll Crowell, renewed © 1980 by Reid Crowell. Reprinted by permission of HarperCollins Publishers, Inc. FROST, ROBERT. "Moon Compasses" from *The Poetry of Robert Frost*, edited by Edward Connery Lathem. Copyright © 1936 by Robert Frost, © 1964 by Lesley Frost Ballantine, © 1969 by Henry Holt and Co. Reprinted by permission of Henry Holt and Company, LLC. STRONG, PATIENCE. "Before You Came" from *Happy Days*. Used by permission of Rupert Crew Limited. Our sincere thanks to the following authors whom we were unable to locate: Charles Jefferys for "We Have Lived and Loved Together"; Raymond Kresensky for "By a Way I Knew Not."

CONTENTS

WHEN WE
MET . . .

THE SECRET

I loved thee, though I told thee not,
Right earlily and long,
Thou wert my joy in every spot,
My theme in every song.

And when I saw a stranger face
Where beauty held the claim,
I gave it, like a secret grace,
The being of thy name.

And all the charms of face or voice
Which I in others see
Are but the recollected choice
Of what I feel for thee.

— JOHN CLARE

I WISH I COULD REMEMBER

I wish I could remember that first day,
First hour, first moment of your meeting me,
If bright or dim the season, it might be
Summer or winter for aught I can say;
So unrecorded did it slip away,
So blind was I to see and to foresee,
So dull to mark the budding of my tree

That would not blossom yet for many a May.
If only I could recollect it, such
A day of days! I let it come and go
As traceless as a thaw of bygone snow;
It seemed to mean so little, meant so much;
If only now I could recall that touch,
First touch of hand in hand—did one but know!
— CHRISTINA ROSSETTI

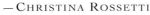

Meeting and Passing

As I went down the hill along the wall
There was a gate I had leaned at for the view
And had just turned from when I first saw you
As you came up the hill. We met. But all
We did that day was mingle great and small
Footprints in summer dust as if we drew
The figure of our being less than two
But more than one as yet. Your parasol
Pointed the decimal off with one deep thrust.
And all the time we talked you seemed to see
Something down there to smile at in the dust.
(Oh, it was without prejudice to me!)
Afterward I went past what you had passed
Before we met and you what I had passed.

— Robert Frost

MOMENTOUS WORDS

What spiteful chance steals unawares
Wherever lovers come,
And trips the nimblest brain and scares
  The bravest feelings dumb?

  We had one minute at the gate,
  Before the others came;
  Tomorrow it would be too late,
  And whose would be the blame!

  I gazed at her, she glanced at me;
Alas! the time sped by:
"How warm it is today!" said she;
"It looks like rain," said I.

—EDWARD ROWLAND SILL

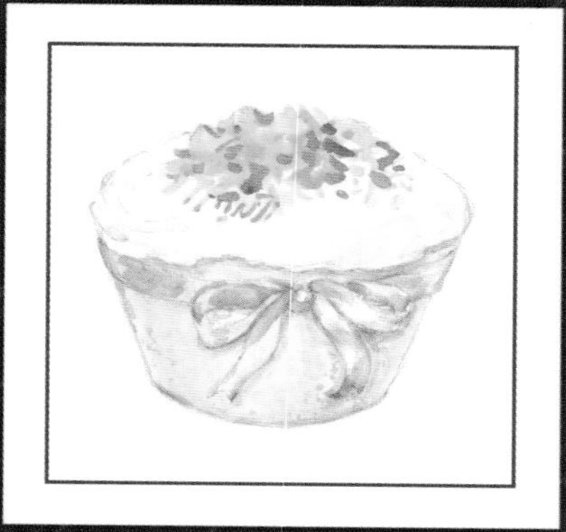

Mood Perfect

We simply walked together,
And not a word was said.
My heart was like a feather
That floated where you led.

We did not touch or whisper,
As lovers often do.
We simply walked together—
It was complete with you.

— Pauline Chadwell

SHALL I COMPARE THEE TO A SUMMER'S DAY?

Shall I compare thee to a summer's day?
Thou art more lovely and more temperate:
Rough winds do shake the darling buds of May,
And summer's lease hath all too short a date:
Sometime too hot the eye of heaven shines,
And often is his gold complexion dimmed;
And every fair from fair sometimes declines,

By chance or nature's changing course untrimmed;
But thy eternal summer shall not fade,
Nor lose possession of that fair thou ow'st;
Nor shall death brag thou wander'st in his shade,
When in eternal lines to time thou grow'st:

    So long as men can breathe, or eyes can see,

    So long lives this, and this gives life to thee.

— WILLIAM SHAKESPEARE

I Taste a Liquor Never Brewed

I taste a liquor never brewed,
From tankards scooped in pearl;
Not all the vats upon the Rhine
Yield such an alcohol!

Inebriate of air am I,
And debauchee of dew,
Reeling, through endless summer days,
From inns of molten blue.

When "landlords" turn the drunken bee
Out of the foxglove's door,
When butterflies renounce their "drams,"
I shall but drink the more!

Till seraphs swing their snowy hats,
And saints to windows run,
To see the little tippler
Leaning against the sun.

— EMILY DICKINSON

SONG

O, it was out by Donnycarney,
When the bat flew from tree to tree,
My love and I did walk together,
And sweet were the words she said to me.

Along with us the summer wind
Went murmuring — O, happily! —
But softer than the breath of summer
Was the kiss she gave to me.

— JAMES JOYCE

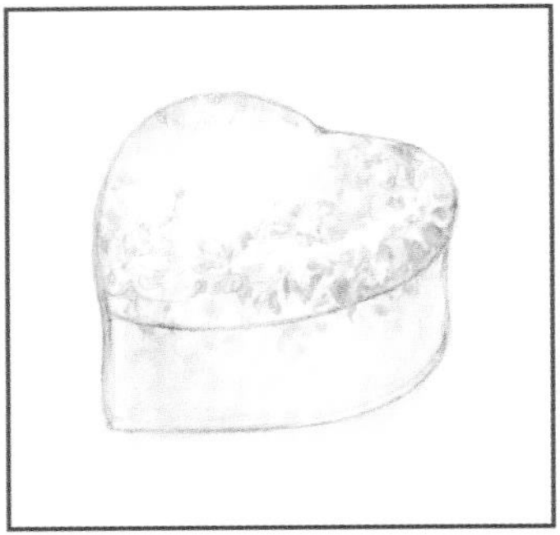

By a Way I Knew Not

I sought afar for loved things
And, wearied, sat to rest.
I saw, but scarcely heeded
You there, so plainly dressed.

I looked into the sunset
And gazed into the sea,
But never spoke my dreaming
Until you spoke to me.

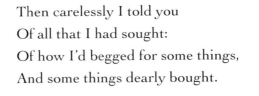

Then carelessly I told you
Of all that I had sought:
Of how I'd begged for some things,
And some things dearly bought.

You listened very calmly,
And laughed a little, too.
I knew that all I sought then,
I found that day in you.
— RAYMOND KRESENSKY

BEFORE YOU CAME

I never heard the songbirds sing
With such a passion of delight.
Nor had I seen, when darkness fell,
The glory of a starry night.

I had not seen the roses bloom,
The morning dew, the sunset flame.
To beauty I was deaf and blind
Before you came, before you came.

I'd never lived, nor did I know
What life could hold of pain and bliss,
And how much happiness could hang
Upon a word, a smile, a kiss.

I did not know that paradise
Could be discovered here below
Before love came into my heart,
But now I know. Yes, now I know.

— PATIENCE STRONG

BE MY
VALENTINE

It's All I Have

It's all I have to bring today,
This, and my heart beside,
This, and my heart, and all the fields,
And all the meadows wide.
Be sure you count, should I forget—
Some one the sum could tell—
This, and my heart, and all the bees
Which in the clover dwell.

— Emily Dickinson

THE QUIET ROAD

Last night I dreamed I walked with you,
Sweetheart of mine,
Along a road that once I knew,
Sweetheart of mine;
A country road where flowers grew,
And sweet red clover, wet with dew,
Green trees with sunshine sifting through;
And over all God's skies of blue.
There hand in hand I walked with you.

Oh, dare I ask you walk with me,
Sweetheart of mine,
Along that quiet road and free,
Sweetheart of mine?

Could you walk ever happily
The road that calls in dreams to me,
  Or would it all too lowly be?
    For orchids grow not there, you see,
    Could you love clover blooms and me,
    Sweetheart?
    — B. Y. WILLIAMS

I Forget All Time

With thee conversing, I forget all time,
All seasons, and their change; all please alike.

Sweet is the breath of morn, her rising sweet,
With charm of earliest birds; pleasant the sun
When first on this delightful land he spreads
His orient beams; on herb, tree, fruit, and flower

Glistering with dew; fragrant the fertile earth
After soft showers, and sweet the coming on
Of grateful evening mild; then silent night,
With this her solemn bird, and this fair moon,
And these the gems of heaven, her starry train.

But neither breath of morn, when she ascends
With charm of earliest birds; nor rising sun
On this delightful land; nor herb, fruit, flower
Glistering with dew; nor fragrance after showers;
Nor grateful evening mild; nor silent night,
With this her solemn bird; nor walk by moon,
Or glittering starlight, without thee is sweet.
—JOHN MILTON

VALENTINE

When I shall have no need for you,
Then I shall have no need
For words of beauty in my heart,
Nor for my soul a creed.

When I shall have no need for you
And all your love can bring,
Then I shall have, my dearest one,
No need for anything.

— MERRY BROWNE

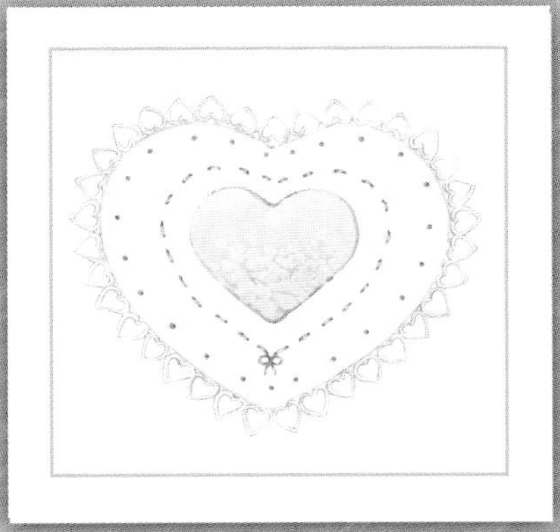

LOVE'S PHILOSOPHY

The fountains mingle with the river,
  And the rivers with the ocean;
The winds of heaven mix forever,
  With a sweet emotion;
Nothing in the world is single;
  All things by a law divine
In one another's being mingle: —
  Why not I with thine?

See! the mountains kiss high heaven,
    And the waves clasp one another;
No sister flower would be forgiven
    If it disdained its brother;
And the sunlight clasps the earth,
    And the moonbeams kiss the sea:—
What are all these kissings worth,
If thou kiss not me?

—PERCY BYSSHE SHELLEY

HE KISSED ME

First time he kissed me, he but only kissed
The fingers of this hand wherewith I write;
And ever since, it grew more clean and white,
Slow to world-greetings, quick with its "Oh, list,"
When the angels speak. A ring of amethyst
I could not wear here, plainer to my sight,
Than that first kiss. The second passed in height
The first, and sought the forehead, and half missed,
Half falling on the hair. O beyond meed!
That was the chrism of love, which love's own crown,
With sanctifying sweetness, did precede.

The third upon my lips was folded down
In perfect, purple state; since when, indeed,
I have been proud and said, "My love, my own."
—ELIZABETH BARRETT BROWNING

Jenny Kissed Me

Jenny kissed me when we met,
Jumping from the chair she sat in.
Time, you thief! who loves to get
Sweets into your list, put that in.
Say I'm weary, say I'm sad;
Say that health and wealth have missed me;
Say I'm growing old, but add—
Jenny kissed me!

—Leigh Hunt

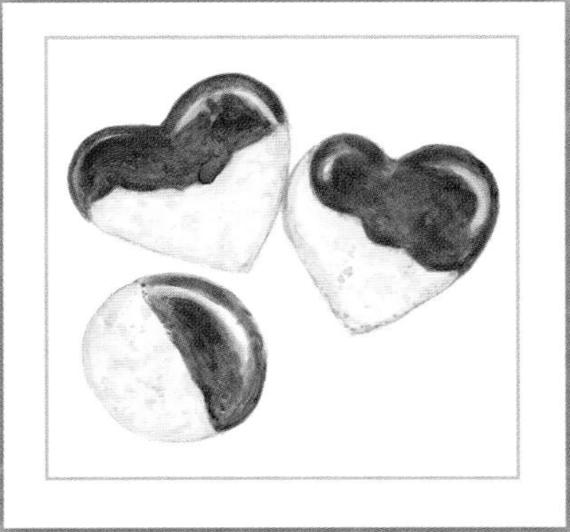

SWEET PERIL

Alas, how easily things go wrong!
A sigh too much, or a kiss too long,
And there follows a mist and a weeping rain,
And life is never the same again.

Alas, how hardly things go right!
'Tis hard to watch in a summer night,
For the sigh will come, and the kiss will stay,
And the summer night is a wintry day.

And yet how easily things go right,
If the sigh and a kiss of a summer's night
Come deep from the soul in the stronger ray
That is born in the light of a winter's day.

And things can never go badly wrong
If the heart be true and the love be strong,
For the mist, if it comes, and the weeping rain
Will be changed by the love into sunshine again.

—GEORGE MACDONALD

A WOMAN'S QUESTION

Do you know you have asked for the costliest thing
Ever made by the Hand above?
 A woman's heart, and a woman's life —
 And a woman's wonderful love.

 Do you know you have asked for this priceless thing
As a child might ask for a toy?
Demanding what others have died to win,
With the reckless dash of a boy.

I am fair and young, but the rose may fade
From my soft young cheek one day;
Will you love me then 'mid the falling leaves,
As you did 'mong the blossoms of May?

I require all things that are grand and true,
All things that a man should be;
If you give this all, I would stake my life
To be all you demand of me.

If you cannot be this, a laundress and cook
You can hire and little to pay;
But a woman's heart and a woman's life
Are not to be won that way.

— LENA LATHROP

YOU AND I

My hand is lonely for your clasping, dear;
    My ear is tired waiting for your call.
I want your strength to help, your laugh to cheer;
    Heart, soul, and senses need you, one and all.
I droop without your full, frank sympathy;
    We ought to be together—you and I;

We want each other so, to comprehend

   The dream, the hope, things planned, or seen, or wrought.

Companion, comforter and guide and friend,

   As much as love asks love, does thought ask thought.

Life is so short, so fast the lone hours fly,

   We ought to be together, you and I.

— HENRY ALFORD

I'll Be True, Valentine

Doubt Not

Doubt that the stars are fire;
Doubt that the sun doth move;
Doubt truth to be a liar;
But never doubt I love.

—William Shakespeare

DOST THOU LOVE ME?

Dost thou love me, my Belovèd?
    Who shall answer yes or no?
What is provèd or disprovèd
    When my soul inquireth so,
Dost thou love me, my Belovèd?

I have seen thy heart to-day,
    Never open to the crowd,
While to love me aye and aye
    Was the vow as it was vowed
By thine eyes of steadfast grey.

Count what feelings used to move me!
    Can this love assort with those?

Thou, who art so far above me,
    Wilt thou stoop so, for repose?
Is it true that thou canst love me?

Do not blame me if I doubt thee.
    I can call love by its name
When thine arm is wrapt about me;
    But even love seems not the same,
When I sit alone, without thee.

Dost thou love me, my Belovèd?
    Only *thou* canst answer yes!
And, thou gone, the proof's disprovèd,
    And the cry rings answerless—
Dost thou love me, my Belovèd?
—ELIZABETH BARRETT BROWNING

LOVE'S NOT TIME'S FOOL

Let me not to the marriage of true minds
Admit impediments. Love is not love
Which alters when it alteration finds,
Or bends with the remover to remove:

Oh, no! It is an ever-fixéd mark,

That looks on tempests and is never shaken;

It is the star to every wandering bark,

Whose worth's unknown, although his height be taken.

Love's not Time's fool, though rosy lips and cheeks

Within his bending sickle's compass come;

Love alters not with his brief hours and weeks,

But bears it out even to the edge of doom.

    If this be error and upon me proved,

      I never writ, nor no man ever loved.

—WILLIAM SHAKESPEARE

FOR LOVE'S SAKE ONLY

If thou must love me, let it be for nought
Except for love's sake only. Do not say
"I love her for her smile—her look—her way
Of speaking gently,—for a trick of thought
That falls in well with mine, and certes brought
A sense of pleasant ease on such a day"—
For these things in themselves, Belovèd, may
Be changed, or change for thee,—and love, so wrought,
May be unwrought so. Neither love me for
Thine own dear pity's wiping my cheeks dry,—
A creature might forget to wep, who bore
Thy comfort long, and lose thy love thereby!
But love me for love's sake, that evermore
Thou mayst love on, through love's eternity.

—ELIZABETH BARRETT BROWNING

FORGET THEE?

"Forget thee?" If to dream by night and muse on thee by day,
If all the worship deep and wild a poet's heart can pay,
If prayers in absence breathed for thee to Heaven's protecting power,
If winged thoughts that flit to thee—a thousand in an hour—
If busy fancy blending thee with all my future lot—
If this thou call'st "forgetting," thou, indeed, shalt be forgot!

"Forget thee?" Bid the forest-birds forget their sweetest tune;
"Forget thee?" Bid the sea forget to swell beneath the moon;
Bid the thirsty flowers forget to drink the eve's refreshing dew;
Thyself forget thine own "dear land," and its "mountains wild and blue."
Forget each old familiar face, each long-remember'd spot—
When these things are forgot by thee, then thou shalt be forgot!

Keep, if thou wilt, thy maiden peace, still calm and fancy-free,

For God forbid thy gladsome heart should grow less glad for me;

Yet, while that heart is still unwon, oh! bid not mine to rove,

But let it nurse its humble faith and uncomplaining love;

If these, preserved for patient years, at last avail me not,

Forget me then; but ne'er believe that thou canst be forgot!

—JOHN MOULTRIE

THE PRESENCE OF LOVE

And in Life's noisiest hour,
There whispers still the ceaseless love of thee,
The heart's self-solace and soliloquy.
You mould my hopes, you fashion me within;
And to the leading love-throb in the heart
Thro' all my being, thro' my pulses beat;

You lie in all my many thoughts like light,
Like the fair light of dawn or summer eve
On rippling stream, or cloud-reflecting lake.
And looking to the heaven, that bends above you,
How oft I bless the lot that made me love you.

—SAMUEL TAYLOR COLERIDGE

I Am of You

Were it wide as the earth
And wild as the sea,
There is nothing, my darlin',
Could keep me from thee.

For I am of you as the bough to the leaf,
As the root to the tree;
No, nothing, my darlin',
Could part me from thee.

—Traditional Irish Ballad

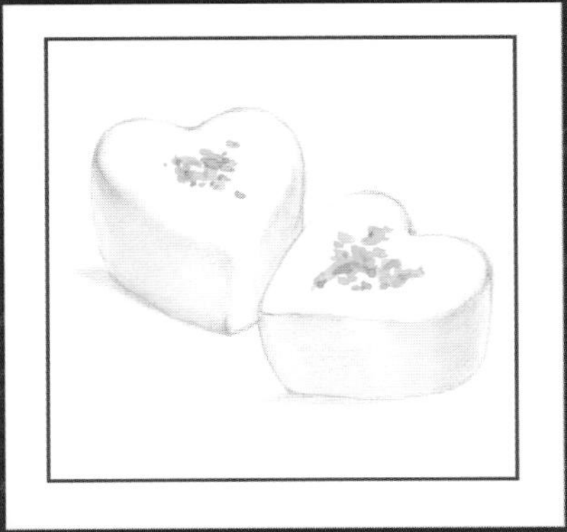

A Woman's Shortcomings

She has laughed as softly as if she sighed,
 She has counted six and over,
Of a purse well filled, and a heart well tried —
 Oh each a worthy lover!
They "give her time"; for her soul must slip
 Where the world has set the grooving:
She will lie to none with her fair red lip —
But love seeks truer loving.

She trembles her fan in a sweetness dumb,
    As her thoughts were beyond recalling,
With a glance for *one,* and a glance for *some,*
    For her eyelids rising and falling;
Speaks common words with a blushful air,
    Hears bold words, unreproving;
But her silence says—what she never will swear—
And love seeks better loving.

Go, lady, lean to the night-guitar,
    And drop a smile to the bringer,
Then smile as sweetly, when he is far,
    At the voice of an indoor singer.

Bask tenderly beneath tender eyes;
Glance lightly on their removing;
And join new vows to old perjuries—
But dare not call it loving.

Unless you can think, when the song is done,
No other is soft in the rhythm;
Unless you can feel, when left by one,
That all men else go with him;
Unless you can know, when unpraised by his breath,
That your beauty itself wants proving;
Unless you can swear, "For life, for death!"—
Oh fear to call it loving!

Unless you can muse in a crowd all day,
    On the absent face that fixed you;
Unless you can love, as the angels may,
    With the breadth of heaven betwixt you;
Unless you can dream that his faith is fast,
    Through behoving and unbehoving;
Unless you can *die* when the dream is past—
    Oh never call it loving!

—Elizabeth Barrett Browning

BE MY LOVE,
VALENTINE

Grow Old Along with Me!

Grow old along with me!
The best is yet to be,
The last of life, for which the first was made:
Our times are in his hand
Who saith: "A whole I planned,
Youth shows but half; trust God, see all, nor be afraid."

— Robert Browning

LOVE ME, SWEET

Love me, sweet, with all thou art,
    Feeling, thinking, seeing,—
Love me in the lightest part,
    Love me in full being.

Love me with thine azure eyes,
    Made for earnest granting!
Taking color from the skies,
    Can Heaven's truth be wanting?

Love me with their lids, that fall
    Snow-like at first meeting:

Love me with thine heart, that all
    The neighbors then see beating.

Love me with thine hand stretched out
    Freely—open-minded:
Love me with thy loitering foot,—
    Hearing one behind it.

Love me with thy voice, that turns
    Sudden faint above me;
Love me with thy blush that burns
    When I murmur "Love me!"

—ELIZABETH BARRETT BROWNING

THE PASSIONATE SHEPHERD TO HIS LOVE

Come live with me and be my love,
And we will all the pleasures prove
That valleys, groves, hills, and fields,
Woods, or steepy mountain yields.

And we will sit upon the rocks,
Seeing the shepherds feed their flocks,
By shallow rivers to whose falls
Melodious birds sing madrigals.

And I will make thee beds of roses
And a thousand fragrant posies,
A cap of flowers, and a kirtle
Embroidered all with leaves of myrtle;

A gown made of the finest wool
Which from our pretty lambs we pull;
Fair lined slippers for the cold,
With buckles of the purest gold;

A belt of straw and ivy buds,
With coral clasps and amber studs:
And if these pleasures may thee move,
Come live with me, and be my love.

The shepherds' swains shall dance and sing
For thy delight each May morning:
If these delights thy mind may move,
Then live with me and be my love.

— CHRISTOPHER MARLOWE

Moon Compasses

I stole forth dimly in the dripping pause
Between two downpours to see what there was.
And a masked moon had spread down compass rays
To a cone mountain in the midnight haze,
As if the final estimate were hers;
And as it measured in her calipers,
The mountain stood exalted in its place.
So love will take between the hands a face. . . .

— Robert Frost

To the One I Love

I Would Not Have Thee Far Away

I would not have thee far away
By whom I must be led.
I needs must have thee every day
To be my meat and bread.

For if there be unlovely things
Wherein no radiance glows,
I'll kiss them till their folded wings
Shall blossom like the rose!

POEMS FOR MY VALENTINE

Oh, be thou beautiful, I'll say—
And save me with delight!
Then each dark thing will smile like day
Between me and the night.

I'll listen till I make them speak,
By need will make them wise!
As love calls blushes to the cheek
Or laughter to the eyes.

For where love lays its trusting kiss
There beauty needs must be
And so I'll turn the world to bliss
Until it shines like thee.
—ANNA HEMPSTEAD BRANCH

WHEN I THINK OF YOU

Dear, when I think of you I too must think
Of things that ever were a part of you,
All glad and beautiful: of open fires,
Of autumn sunlight melting through the blue
Clear sky upon the yellow fallen leaves,
Of books, and rare old paintings and of flowers,
Of starlight, and of moonlight, and of songs
Well-sung that glorify the common hours.

And dear, I find that when I think of you
My thoughts are freed from all things false and wrong.
My being is uplifted like as one
Who in some dim cathedral hears the song

And prayer of unseen suppliants, and there,
Exalted with a new sweet sense of true
And better things, may go away transformed.
So dear, my thoughts are when I think of you.

—GRACE NOLL CROWELL

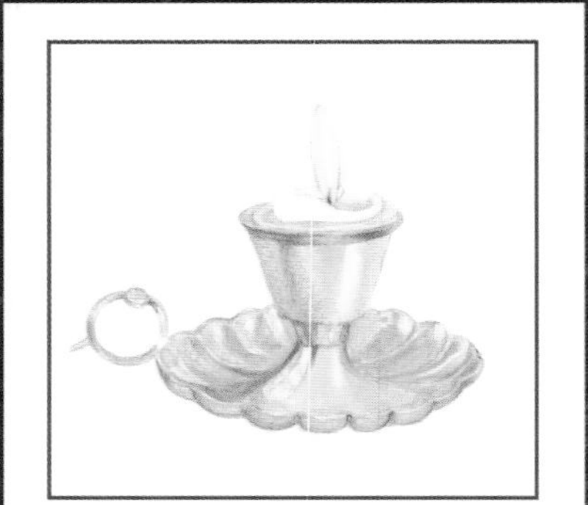

How Do I Love Thee?

How do I love thee? Let me count the ways.
I love thee to the depth and breadth and height
My soul can reach, when feeling out of sight
For the ends of Being and ideal Grace.
I love thee to the level of everyday's
Most quiet need, by sun and candle-light.
I love thee freely, as men strive for Right;
I love thee purely, as they turn from Praise.
I love thee with the passion put to use
In my old griefs, and with my childhood's faith.
I love thee with a love I seemed to lose
With my lost saints, — I love thee with the breath,
Smiles, tears, of all my life! — and, if God choose,
I shall but love thee better after death.

— Elizabeth Barrett Browning

A CUP OF TEA

Nellie made a cup of tea,
Made and poured it out for me,
And above the steaming brew
Smiled and asked me, "One or two?"
Saucily she tossed her head;
"Make it sweet for me," I said.

Two sweet lumps of sugar fell
Into that small china well,
But I knew the while I drained
Every drop the cup contained,
More than sugar in the tea
Made the beverage sweet for me.

This to her I tried to say
In that golden yesterday—
Life is like a cup of tea
Which time poureth endlessly,
Brewed by trial's constant heat
Needing love to make it sweet.

Then I caught her looking up,
And I held my dainty cup
Out to her and bravely said,
"Here is all that lies ahead;
Here is all my life to be—
Will you make it sweet for me?"
—Author Unknown

WE HAVE LIVED AND LOVED TOGETHER

We have lived and loved together
    Through many changing years;
We have shared each other's gladness
    And wept each other's tears;
I have known ne'er a sorrow
    That was long unsoothed by thee;
For thy smiles can make a summer
    Where darkness else would be.

Like the leaves that fall around us
    In autumn's fading hours,
Are the traitor's smiles, that darken
    When the cloud of sorrow lowers;

And though many such we've known, love,
    Too prone, alas, to range,
We both can speak of one love
    Which time can never change.

We have lived and loved together
    Through many changing years;
We have shared each other's gladness
    And wept each other's tears.
And let us hope the future,
    As the past has been will be:

    I will share with thee my sorrows,
    And thou thy joys with me.
—CHARLES JEFFERYS

LOVE'S REASON

For that thy face is fair I love thee not;
Nor yet because the light of thy brown eyes
Hath gleams of wonder and of glad surprise,
Like woodland streams that cross a sunlit spot:
Nor for thy beauty, born without a blot,
Most perfect when it shines through no disguise
Pure as the star of Eve in Paradise, —
For all these outward things I love thee not:

But for a something in thy form and face,
Thy looks and ways, of primal harmony;
A certain soothing charm, a vital grace
That breathes of the eternal womanly,
And makes me feel the warmth of Nature's breast,
When in her arms, and thine, I sink to rest.

— HENRY VAN DYKE

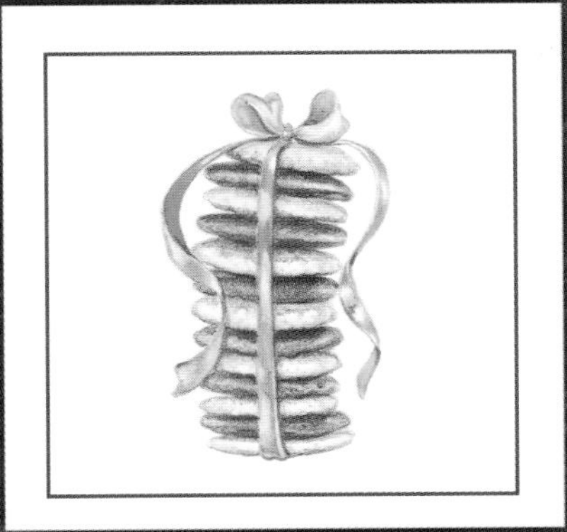

WILL YOU LOVE ME WHEN I'M OLD?

I would ask of you, my darling,
    A question soft and low,
That gives me many a heartache
    As the moments come and go.

Your love I know is truthful,
    But the truest love grows cold;
It is this that I would ask you:
    Will you love me when I'm old?
        Life's morn will soon be waning,
           And its evening bells be tolled,
        But my heart shall know no sadness,
           If you'll love me when I'm old.

Down the stream of life together
    We are sailing side by side,

Hoping some bright day to anchor
  Safe beyond the surging tide.
Today our sky is cloudless,
  But the night may clouds unfold;
But, though storms may gather round us,
  Will you love me when I'm old?

When my hair shall shade the snowdrift,
  And mine eyes shall dimmer grow,
I would lean upon some loved one,
  Through the valley as I go.
I would claim of you a promise,
  Worth to me a world of gold;
It is only this, my darling,
  That you'll love me when I'm old.

—AUTHOR UNKNOWN

Meeting at Night

The gray sea and the long black land;
And the yellow half-moon large and low;
And the startled little waves that leap
In fiery ringlets from their sleep,
As I gain the cove with pushing prow,
And quench its speed i' the slushy sand.

Then a mile of warm sea-scented beach;
Three fields to cross till a farm appears;
A tap at the pane, the quick sharp scratch
And blue spurt of a lighted match,
And a voice less loud, through its joys and fears,
Than the two hearts beating each to each!

— Robert Browning

TITLE INDEX

First Line Index

POEMS FOR MY VALENTINE

FIRST LINE INDEX

AUTHOR INDEX

...do shake the darling buds of

...: sometime too hot the eye of

...dimmed; and every fair from

...changing course untrimmed; be

...at fair thou ow'st; nor shall

...ternal lines to time thou grow

...long lives this, and this gi...

...ou art more lovely and more